This is my gift to you to wish you the merriest Christmas ever!
These coupons never expire and are redeemable at any time.

To:

From:

Published by Sourcebooks, Inc.
P.O. Box 4410, Naperville, Illinois 60567–4410
(630) 961–3900
Fax: (630) 961–2168
www.sourcebooks.com

ISBN-13: 978-1-4022-2007-4
ISBN-10: 1–4022-2007-3

Printed and bound in the United States of America
SP 10 9 8 7 6 5 4 3 2 1

Coupons from Santa

Stocking stuffer coupons to redeem throughout the year!

Sweet Tooth

I'm baking a batch of cookies—
any kind; it's your choice!

Watch What You Wish
Santa's giving you control
of the remote today.

Endless Christmas

Redeem for one gift from Santa.

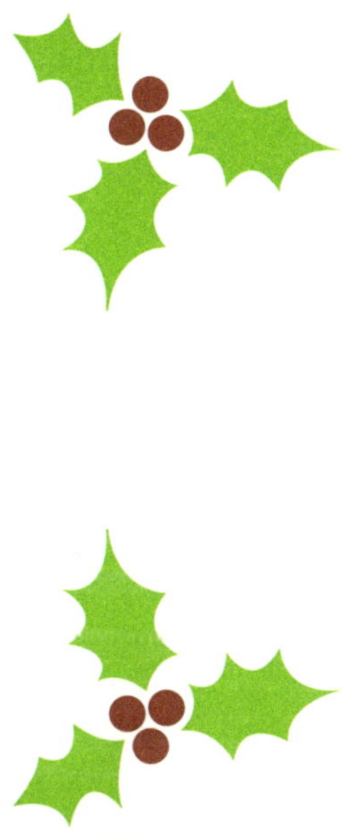

Helping Hand

Today I'll help you out with whatever you want.

Breakfast in Bed

From me to you.

MASSAGE
Good for one back rub.

Endless Christmas

Can't wait 'til next year to watch your favorite Christmas movie? Redeem this, and we'll watch it tonight!

Garbage Time

Santa's taking out the garbage today.

And the recycling, too.

NEW TUNES

Santa will bring you one new album of your choice.

Peace and Quiet

I'll leave you alone for an hour while you take some quiet time for yourself to read, nap, or do whatever you want.

Endless Christmas

Tonight I'll cook your favorite dish for "Christmas" dinner.

SPEED RACER

Know who's washing your car today?

You guessed it—Santa!

Ice Cream Sundae

Let's make sundaes—
you pick the toppings!

Snuggle Bunny
Redeem for one great big hug.

Endless Christmas

In the Christmas spirit, I'll make a donation in your name to the charity of your choice.

Pizza Your Way

Santa says you can pick the toppings tonight.

Maid for an Hour

You choose the chore, and I will happily do it for you.

A Night at the Movies
Any movie you want, tickets on me!

Endless Christmas

'Tis always the season for hot chocolate! This cup comes with whipped cream, marshmallows, and a candy cane garnish.

Santa Says No Fighting

Use this during any argument and you're automatically the winner!

Bon Appétit

You pick the menu, and I'll do all the cooking. If I can't cook it, I'll take you out.

Santa Loves You

He's going to leave you a letter listing all the reasons you're so special.